Whales

PHOTOS AND FACTS FOR EVERYONE

BY ISIS GAILLARD

Learn With Facts Series

Book 73

Dedicated to my boys Jaxon and Jalen

CONTENTS

Isis Gaillard. Whales: Photos and Fun Facts for Kids (Kids Learn With Pictures Series Book 82). Ebook Edition.
Learn With Facts an imprint of TLM Media LLC

eISBN: 978-1-63497-199-7
ISBN-13: 978-1-63497-326-7

Introduction

Whales are part of the scientific order Cetacean, which means they are aquatic mammals with two forelimbs in the form of fins, a tail with horizontal flukes, and a blowhole at the top of their heads from which they breathe. Being mammals means they are warm-blooded and must breathe air, hence their blowholes for easy access.

Whales are among the world's largest animals and include a variety of different types divided into two subcategories: Baleen Whales, which have mouth plates that filter food from water, and Toothed Whales that hunt and catch other marine animals for food.

Whales can be found in every ocean around the world, and while some migrate throughout the seven seas, certain whales will stay within relatively small areas of the world's oceans. Bowheads, for example, are the only whales that spend their entire lives in Arctic waters near either the North or South poles. True to their name, the North Atlantic right whale migrates up and down the east coast of America and the western coasts of Spain, France, Great Britain, and Norway. In contrast, the Grey Whale is concentrated only along the western U.S. coast and the eastern coast of Asia. Regardless of whether they stay concentrated in a particular region or circumnavigate the globe, whales populate all of the earth's saltwater environments.

Description

Whales can communicate with each other across great distances through vocalization. The sounds they make vary from the deep rhythmic songs of the Humpback to the rapid, chattering clicks of Beluga whales. Like all of the Toothed Whales, Belugas uses echolocation through vocalization to find food, openings in ice sheets through which to breathe, and for identification. This echolocation is accomplished through a structure in all Toothed whale heads called the melon. It is believed that the melon absorbs sound waves that bounce off of objects when the whale vocalizes. This absorption, in turn, allows the whale to pinpoint the location of the object.

Like humans, whales are very social animals. They are known to teach and learn from each other, hunt together, and even grieve the loss of a social group member. Studies of the whale's brain show a similarity to that of certain areas of the human brain responsible for socialization and communication. This, in turn, may explain why whales in captivity have been known to mimic human vocalization in an attempt to communicate with us.

Breaching is common among most whale species by where the animal propels itself upward to break out of the surface of the water. The reasons for breaching can range from a display of dominance among males in a social group to stunning prey with a loud slap of the water's surface when they come down. Another common reason may be to dislodge parasites from the whale's body that accumulate while underwater.

Many whales like the Humpback and Blues are migratory, meaning they travel great distances for the year. This behavior can be attributed to the need to follow the migration of specific foods and the need to return to certain breeding/birthing grounds

Certain whales from the Baleen and Toothed categories have developed peculiar hunting techniques that depend upon their environment. Humpbacks incorporate the technique of "bubble netting" by which they emit bubbles while swimming in an ever-tightening circle below their prey. The bubbles group and push prey towards the surface where the whales simultaneously emerge, mouths opened wide, to swallow thousands of fish in a single "net." Orcas are the only whales that will intentionally beach themselves to catch prey as they chase it onto the shore. Orcas will also work in groups to create massive waves that can wash prey off of floating icebergs.

Size

Baleen Whales:

Taking first place as the largest animal in the world is the Blue Whale, which averages almost 100 feet in length and can weigh 170 tons. The Blue whale has a long tapering body, which is in contrast to that of most other whale species.

Toothed Whales

The largest of all toothed whales is the sperm whale, weighing around 50 tons. This whale has a very distinctive block-shaped head that can make up over ¼ of its total body length. Its lower jaw is very long and narrow and contains all of the whale's teeth.

Breeding

Reproduction is quite similar between Baleen and Toothed whales. All females or "cows" give birth to a single "calf." Generally, females will calve once every three to five years, although the sperm whale has been known to wait as long as 20 years between offspring. Male or "bull" whales are highly competitive with each other over a single female, and one cow may have several mates during a single breeding season. The timing of breeding season varies depending on whale; some whales, like Orcas, may breed and calve at any time of the year, similar to humans.

Gestation lengths also vary from 10 – 15 months depending on the type and the amount of time the calf stays with its mother may be from 6 months to a full year. Finally, while males generally do not participate in the offspring's parental care, many different whale species have been known to share the responsibility within groups of females and juveniles.

Eating Habit

Baleen whales consume mainly krill, which are very small, shrimp-like crustaceans. Although they are nearly invisible to the naked eye, krill populations make up biomass nearly twice that of the human population at over 500 million tons. Because of this enormous biomass, the largest whales of the world make krill the mainstay of their diets. Baleens are also known to consume large schools of smaller fish such as Mackerel.

Eating Habit

Toothed whales have a much wider variety of food choices. Sperm whales are highly adapted to hunting gigantic squid that lives at extreme depths. Beluga whales are more opportunistic feeders consuming whatever fish and other marine animals are most abundant at different times. Killer whales do not just stop hunting any type of fish but also feed on marine mammals such as seals and even other whales.

Interesting Facts

1. A whale is a Cetaceans that evolved from terrestrial (land) mammals!

2. Since cetaceans are mammals, they breathe air. They come on land or ice to reproduce and breed.

3. Whales are the largest animals to have ever lived – even larger than any dinosaur!

4. Whales have the longest migrations of any mammal.

5. Sound and communication are incredibly important to life in the ocean!

6. Cetaceans play an important role in the food web by keeping the ocean ecosystem balanced and healthy.

7. Whales help to reduce climate change with their poop.

THE END

Thanks for reading facts about Whales. I am a parent of two boys on the autism spectrum. I am always advocating for Autism Spectrum Disorders which part of the proceeds of this book goes to many Non-Profit Autism Organizations. I would love if you would leave a review.

Author Note from Isis Gaillard:

Thanks For Reading! I hope you enjoyed the fact book about Whales.

Please check out all the Learn With Facts and the Kids Learn With Pictures series available.

Visit www.IsisGaillard.com and www.LearnWithFacts.com to find more books in the Learn With Facts Series

More Books In The Series

Over 75 books in the Learn With Facts Series.

Set 1

```
A  L  L  X  R  F  K  Y  S  A  S  I  X  K  P
S  Q  H  Y  N  O  W  O  G  R  B  G  S  O  W
E  L  X  D  B  X  O  B  A  I  A  D  O  R  R
L  G  W  B  Z  E  U  Y  T  L  R  G  F  R  D
E  K  G  O  O  S  B  X  Z  I  A  V  U  U  F
P  L  D  W  H  I  E  H  B  E  I  S  Y  O  S
H  S  D  V  I  C  E  C  T  E  Y  W  C  H  C
A  C  H  I  N  C  H  I  L  L  A  S  A  I  J
N  S  S  B  N  N  F  A  F  J  L  T  Y  A  L
T  O  E  U  T  O  F  P  M  V  E  D  C  I  S
S  O  D  S  M  F  S  V  T  E  R  S  O  W  R
E  R  Z  O  R  A  G  A  H  Y  L  N  Q  V  A
A  A  F  E  L  O  T  C  U  I  S  E  Q  Y  E
G  G  Q  R  G  P  H  O  K  R  A  K  O  L  B
L  N  T  C  X  X  H  Z  P  F  S  E  A  N  B
E  A  L  I  S  E  L  I  D  O  C  O  R  C  S
S  K  D  E  K  V  W  S  N  D  P  N  D  Z  I
S  G  O  H  E  G  D  E  H  S  O  P  F  G  I
F  H  S  R  E  V  A  E  B  P  C  C  I  B  S
A  H  B  P  E  G  I  R  A  F  F  E  S  H  E
```

Word List

Bears	Dolphins	Kangaroos
Beavers	Eagles	Koalas
Birds	Elephants	Lions
Chameleons	Foxes	Owls
Cheetahs	Frogs	
Chinchillas	Giraffes	
Cougars	Hedgehogs	
Crocodiles	Hippopotamus	
Dinosaurs	Horses	

Set 2

```
Z G K M V B E E S S O V E E P
P E A C O C K S F R A N E Y H
G I P Z A L L I G A T O R S B
C J G A E N F V S U U L Y C R
Y R R U N L X Z R G Q K C S C
H S I F A D L Y E A N O E I K
R P C D H N A E G J T I P H S
H I F A N W A S I X P O X N S
I D Z A M A P S T P Q I E A Y
N E F L H E S B U X T T R G H
O R L P G M L P T O T B B S S
C S A A U M D S A I E A L E I
E A M C E N W S K Z T C R A F
R A I A A U N D M S R T W T Y
O L N S S I N K S E F F V U L
S J G Z U A V E N R R T K R L
G O O G S O C B A H S I A T E
D I N T F C B Y K Q Z C B L J
B E A Q B U T T E R F L I E S
P C I N S E C T S E V Q K S Z
```

Word List

Alligators
Alpacas
Bats
Bees
Butterflies
Camels
Cats and Kittens
Dogs and Puppies
Fish

Flamingo
Gazelle
Hyena
Iguanas
Insects
Jaguars
Jellyfish
Pandas
Peacocks

Penguins
Rhinoceros
Sea Turtles
Snakes
Spiders
Tigers
Zebras

Set 3

```
P  S  G  U  K  P  O  N  I  E  S  C  M  M  S
O  A  N  S  O  C  T  O  P  U  S  E  S  I  E
T  T  R  O  E  R  O  O  S  T  E  R  S  Q  A
C  S  K  R  I  F  K  K  J  M  Y  P  W  S  L
M  Y  J  A  O  P  O  V  J  L  C  I  A  G  S
W  K  C  Q  E  T  R  W  E  S  U  G  N  G  A
H  Z  E  F  I  Y  S  O  R  A  V  S  S  O  N
W  O  L  V  E  S  P  A  C  E  S  A  S  S  D
L  G  Y  Z  W  A  E  S  S  Y  N  W  T  S
V  X  T  L  R  B  D  O  N  D  O  D  N  R  E
H  G  I  D  R  R  O  A  Y  G  S  P  S  I  A
W  E  S  A  A  M  C  G  A  T  T  I  E  C  L
U  H  L  Z  X  I  G  R  P  A  A  G  A  H  I
L  O  I  E  L  T  D  E  K  B  R  L  H  E  O
P  L  O  E  X  O  U  R  I  S  F  E  O  S  N
L  N  P  Q  D  A  E  R  D  G  I  T  R  N  S
B  R  P  O  V  E  S  W  T  X  S  S  S  V  S
A  E  M  L  M  L  Y  N  X  L  H  T  E  W  G
D  O  O  X  X  O  W  H  A  L  E  S  S  H  M
K  V  R  A  N  T  E  A  T  E  R  S  A  J  T
```

Word List

Anteater
Komodo Dragons
Leopards
Lizards
Lynx
Meerkat
Moose
Octopuses
Ostriches

Parrots
Pelicans
Pigs and Piglets
Polar Bears
Ponies
Roosters
Scorpions
Seahorses
Seals and Sea Lions

Starfish
Swans
Turtles
Whales
Wolves

Set 4

```
Z  P  O  R  C  U  P  I  N  E  S  C  M  F  Z
P  K  N  S  K  C  E  O  Y  U  H  A  O  A  I
E  C  H  I  D  N  A  R  F  M  O  E  U  A  H
K  H  C  K  W  Q  E  E  S  E  R  R  N  K  F
R  M  P  L  S  E  U  K  Y  G  O  A  T  S  X
N  A  R  L  D  Q  R  J  N  E  C  H  A  P  V
S  H  C  N  A  O  U  U  G  B  H  P  I  B  L
T  Y  I  C  T  T  P  I  U  B  I  L  N  B  I
C  E  E  S  O  F  Y  F  R  E  C  T  L  Z  V
R  O  G  K  E  O  F  P  Z  R  K  D  I  S  E
F  D  W  I  N  A  N  L  U  R  E  O  O  L  D
E  W  I  S  L  O  G  S  L  S  N  L  N  O  N
R  E  T  O  V  V  D  X  U  A  S  G  S  T  A
R  C  H  I  P  M  U  N  K  S  M  W  W  H  I
E  W  S  H  A  R  K  S  D  Q  S  A  M  S  N
T  I  D  Y  C  Z  O  O  T  H  O  R  A  D  A
S  Y  T  E  G  U  I  N  E  A  P  I  G  S  M
J  S  E  T  E  S  E  E  R  D  L  O  J  T  S
J  K  H  H  F  R  P  S  K  U  N  K  S  N  A
X  A  R  M  A  D  I  L  L  O  C  E  R  L  T
```

Word List

Armadillo	Ferrets	Sharks
Buffalo	Goats	Sheep
Chickens	Guinea Pigs	Skunks
Chipmunks	Llama	Sloths
Cows	Mountain Lions	Squirrels
Deer	Platypus	Storks
Donkeys	Porcupines	Tasmanian Devil
Echidna	Raccoons	
Emu	Reindeer	

Set 5

```
3 W M S E S I O T R O T T X M
0 Q M A R S U P I A L S S S V
D B G Z R J A D D G V B C E A
A A V V H I S L A M M A M T N
N S L A M I N A M R A F S O T
G B J B K X S E Y O X R M Y E
E G A E T U X K L P X I U O L
R P U M R N C F S I C C S C O
O C U L O A O L R B F T S F P
U M A F T J E U S V R E O Y E
S W V T F S I R B A E I P A S
A C L M A I U U M D P J O A A
N E X E I M N P A N T H E R S
I M W G E M H S I T I H B D G
M X T L P I Y F B U L T N V R
A J A D B G A S Q R E B C A L
L T D I Y B K N R K S Q W R B
S P A P V O S O J E S W F K D
U N V B N O D L G Y S J V S Y
S J G O R I L L A S A S A E H
```

Word List

30 Dangerous Animals
Aardvarks
Amphibians
Antelopes
Cattle
Coyotes
Farm Animals
Gorillas
Lemurs

Mammals
Marine Life
Marsupials
Opossums
Panthers
Puffins
Reptiles
Tortoises
Turkeys

Walrus
Weasels
Yaks

Set 1

Set 2

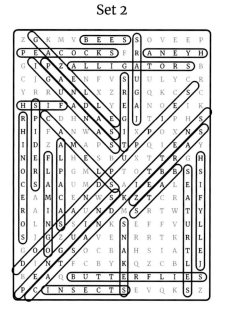

Set 3

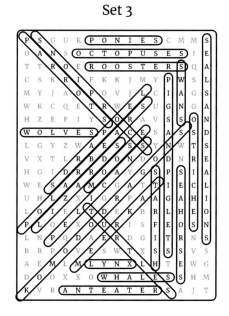

Set 4

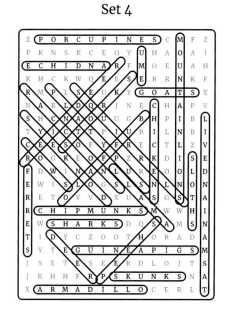

Set 5

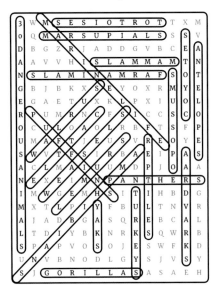

Puzzle 1

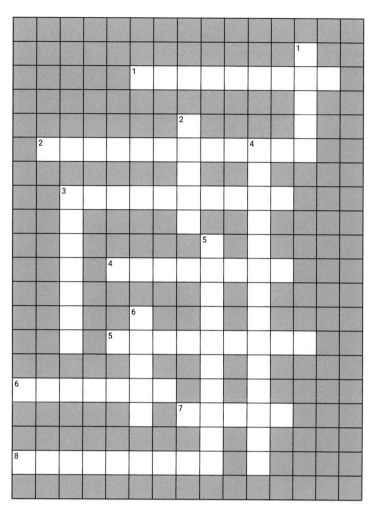

ACROSS
1. Dinosaurs
2. Caterpillars
3. Crocodiles
4. Dolphins
5. Hedgehogs
6. Beavers
7. Foxes
8. Elephants

DOWN
1. Frogs
2. Birds
3. Cougars
4. Apes and Monkeys
5. Chameleons
6. Bears

Puzzle 2

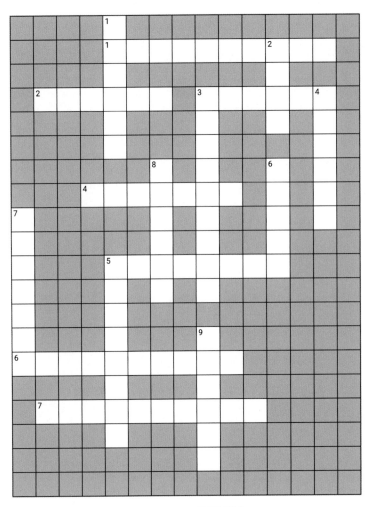

ACROSS
1. Alligators
2. Tigers
3. Koalas
4. Alpacas
5. Peacocks
6. Sea Turtles
7. Rhinoceros

DOWN
1. Camels
2. Owls
3. Kangaroos
4. Snakes
5. Penguins
6. Lions
7. Spiders
8. Pandas
9. Zebras

Puzzle 3

ACROSS
1. Meerkat
2. Lizards
3. Fish
4. Parrots
5. Hyena
6. Leopards
7. Iguanas
8. Gazelle
9. Insects

DOWN
1. Jellyfish
2. Jaguars
3. Ostriches
4. Octopuses
5. Bats
6. Flamingo
7. Moose
8. Lynx

Puzzle 4

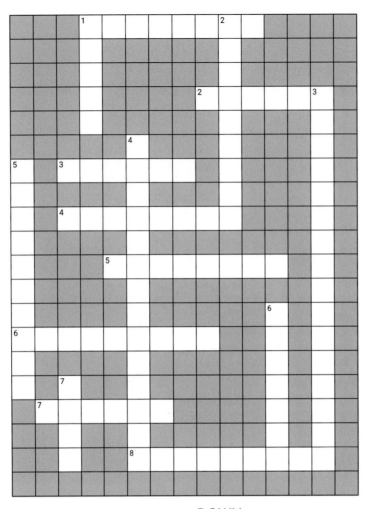

ACROSS
1. Starfish
2. Whales
3. Ponies
4. Roosters
5. Anteater
6. Armadillo
7. Wolves
8. Scorpions

DOWN
1. Swans
2. Seahorses
3. Seals and Sea Lions
4. Pigs and Piglets
5. Polar Bears
6. Buffalo
7. Cows

Puzzle 5

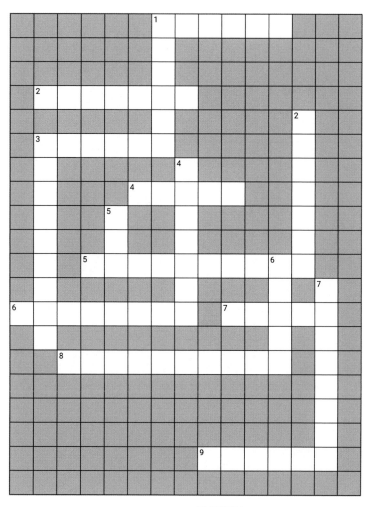

ACROSS
1. Sloths
2. Echidna
3. Storks
4. Sheep
5. Guinea Pigs
6. Platypus
7. Llama
8. Porcupines
9. Sharks

DOWN
1. Skunks
2. Donkeys
3. Squirrels
4. Ferrets
5. Emu
6. Goats
7. Raccoons

Puzzle 6

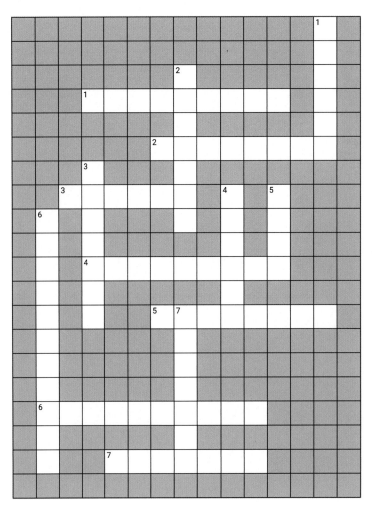

ACROSS
1. Tortoises
2. Gorillas
3. Cattle
4. Aardvarks
5. Opossums
6. Amphibians
7. Weasels

DOWN
1. Lemurs
2. Coyotes
3. Mammals
4. Walrus
5. Yaks
6. Farm Animals
7. Puffins

Puzzle 1

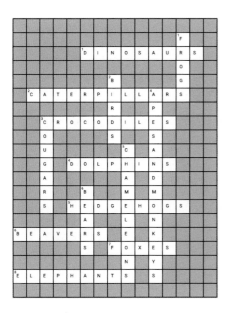

Puzzle 2

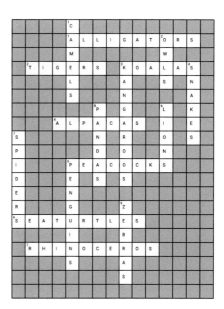

Puzzle 3

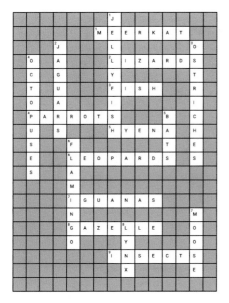

Puzzle 4

Puzzle 5

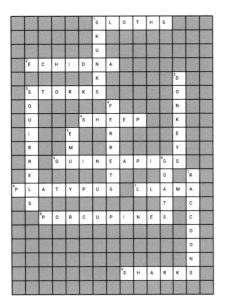

Puzzle 6